BUT...

WHaT ABOUT Me!

HOW IT FeeLS
TO Be a KiD iN DiVORCE

By

BONNIE DOSS

Illustrations by

JENNIFER SCHROEDER

ISBN 0-9653895-8-8

Published by:

BOOKMARK *Publishing*

P.O. Box 270636
Corpus Christi, TX 78427-0636
Phone: 512-992-5814
Fax: 512-994-1593
E-Mail: bk@bookmarkpublishing.com
Website: http://www.bookmarkpublishing.com

ISBN 0-9653895-7-X Hardcover
ISBN 0-9653895-8-8 Softcover

ENDORSEMENTS

"Should be <u>must</u> reading for every divorcing parent!"

> Danny Tower
> Attorney at Law

"This book will help parents see how divorce is experienced by the child and is an added bonus for use in our court mandated divorce course.   It gives the child a tool to express and resolve feelings caused by the divorce."

> Mary Jackson, M.A., LPC
> Executive Director
> Family Counseling Service

"I wish I'd had something like this when I went through my divorce with my children."

> Louise McDonald
> Divorced parent of three children

"This excellent book can help parents and children get in touch with their own feelings and thus promote growth toward a healthier parent/child relationship! *But... What About Me!* is now being offered as an addition to in-service training. The Family Outreach MOMS Group (Mothers Offer Mutual Support) has requested that it be used in their group to help them better understand their children's feelings."

> Linda Isaacs
> Executive Secretary/Volunteer
> Family Outreach, Inc.

"*But... What About Me!* should be read by all **parents** who are divorcing. Too often children in a divorcing family are 'misplaced,' and their feelings are not considered as part of the entire picture... Parents are so 'tangled up' in their own world of anger and the urge to 'win' and 'punish' that they quite often ignore their children's emotional needs. *But... What About Me!* is an excellent example for parents to read... a positive guide for divorcing parents."

> Jack E. Hunter, Judge
> 94th District Court
> Nueces County, Texas

FOREWORD

But... What About Me! How It Feels To Be a Kid in Divorce definitely expresses a child's point of view. I could identify beautifully with the material as a child. I found myself slipping back into my own childhood.

In working with young children in the field of education, I have found it very difficult to find material that has been developed for use with children that is actually written on a child's level.

Many of the problems encountered as an educator of troubled children are a direct result of discord between the parents and their inability to *hear* their children. The expressions and emotions presented here can enable a young child to find his/her own words to identify his/her feelings. This awareness can be a source of comfort in the realization that other children have those same feelings.

This material my successfully be used as a tool in working with children of various ages . Because of the powerful nature of the information, it may be necessary to break it into a number of sessions depending on the age of the child. The illustrations, in additions to expressing the vast array of emotions the child experiences, also work well in the use of art therapy.

But...What About Me! How It Feels To Be a Kid in Divorce is provocative enough for a sixteen year old, easily read by an eight year old and easily understood by a five year old.

In addition, **seeing** the words of children may be one of the most powerful means by which to reach parents. It may well be the least intimidating means of parental confrontation available.

Joyce Spindle, Ph.D.
Founder, Corpus Christi Counseling
and Learning Center

INTRODUCTION

The material in this book represents the deep feelings of a child experiencing the trauma of the break up of his/her family. It does not promote or oppose divorce. It is meant as a tool to help children cope and express themselves at a time when perhaps it might be most difficult. Written and illustrated in words and drawings with which a child can easily identify, it helps the child give voice to his/her feelings and lets the child know that he/she is not the only one to experience those feelings.

The child in the book takes the reader by the hand and leads him/her through the passage way into the child's fears and emotions. Precisely because *But...What About Me!* is written from a child's perspective, it is a non-intimidating, but effective means by which to reach parents, grandparents and other adults affected by divorce. It is especially powerful when read by parents contemplating and/or experiencing divorce or separation. The vast majority of parents do not want to deprive, harm or otherwise injure their children. However, in dealing with their own incredible pain and/or resentments, parents are unable to see beyond their own grief much of the time. It may be difficult for parents to see from the child's point of view, preventing them from being aware of what the child is experiencing. This small book, with its expressive illustrations, helps parents better understand the emotions of their child who also is going through the same divorce or separation. This understanding can enhance communication between parent and child and provide a basis for further dialog.

But...What About Me! is also effective as a tool for counselors working with children who are struggling to cope with divorce or separation. Its direct, childlike language makes it easier for counselors to assist children in exploring their emotions, while the simple illustrations serve as an excellent tool for art therapy.

Additional information on counseling services, parenting classes and community service agencies can be found in telephone directories, libraries, and newspapers. Also, many churches offer counseling or provide referral services.

WHY CAN'T MY MAMA AND DADDY BE TOGETHER? MY FRIENDS HAVE THEIR MAMA AND DADDY AT HOME. WHY CAN'T I?

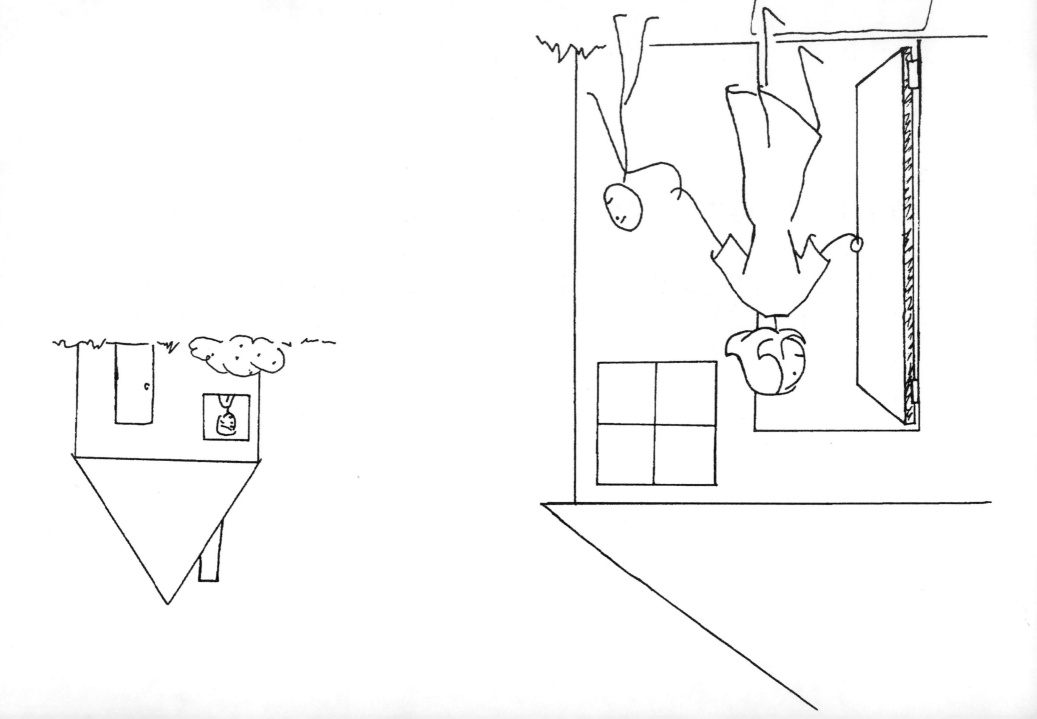

DADDY WASN'T BAD, NOT REALLY. I DON'T UNDERSTAND WHY MAMA DOESN'T LIKE HIM ANYMORE. SHE USED TO LIKE HIM. BUT NOW HE HAS TO LIVE AWAY. WHY DOES MY DADDY HAVE TO LEAVE? I STILL LIKE MY DADDY.

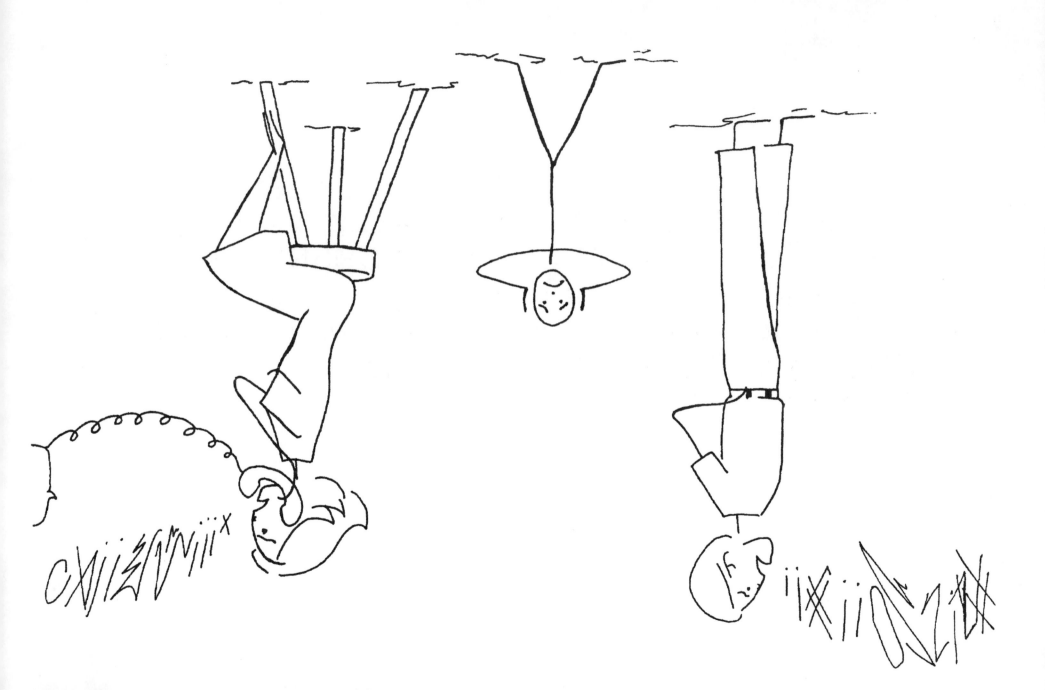

NOW MY MAMA DOESN'T TALK TO MY DADDY, AND MY DADDY SAYS BAD THINGS ABOUT MY MAMA. I HEARD MY MAMA TALKING ON THE PHONE THE OTHER DAY WHEN SHE DIDN'T KNOW I WAS ANYWHERE AROUND, AND SHE WASN'T SAYING NICE THINGS ABOUT DADDY EITHER.

I DON'T KNOW WHERE I'M GOING TO LIVE NOW. AND, PEOPLE ARE ALWAYS ASKING ME THINGS I DON'T LIKE TO TALK ABOUT.

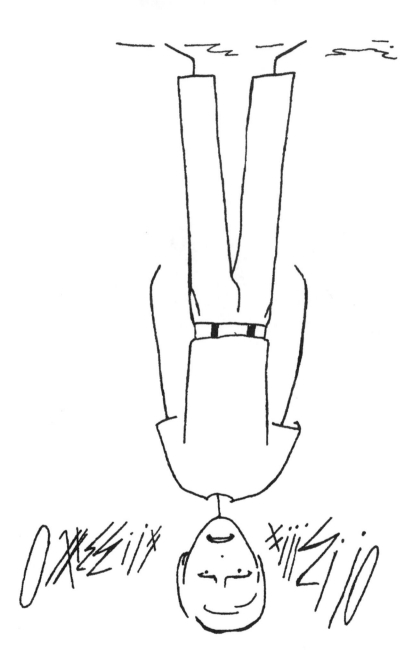

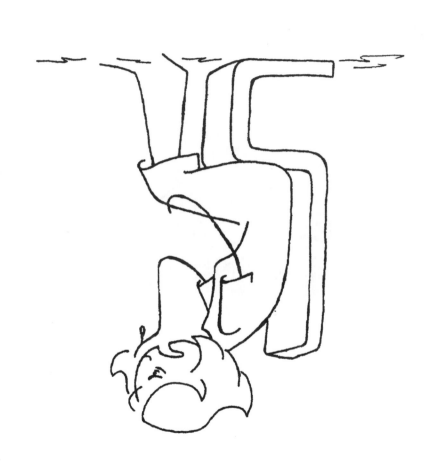

I HeaR MaMa CRY a LOT, aND DaDDY USeS BaD WORDS.

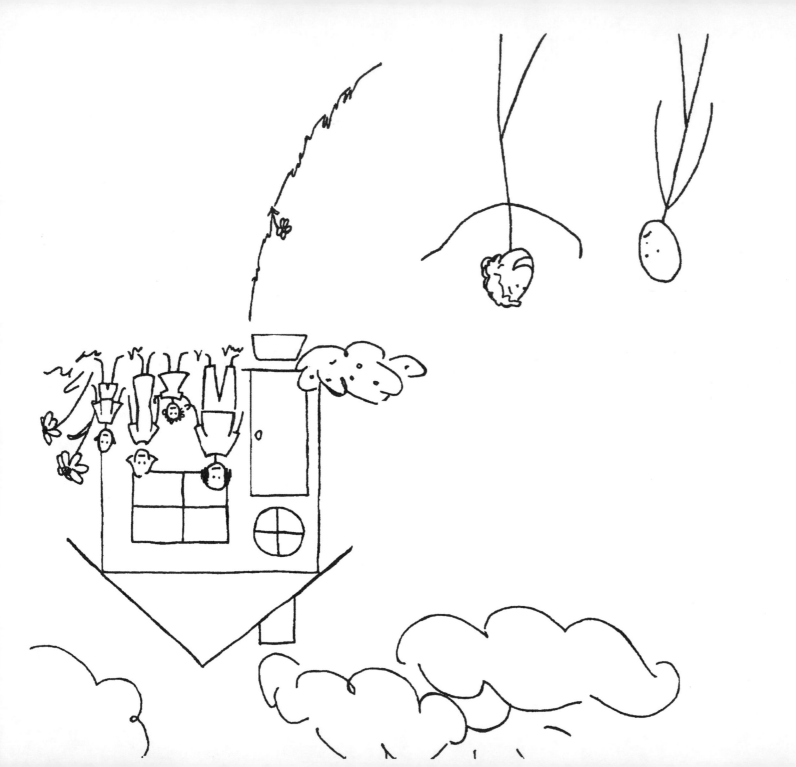

I THINK I WANT TO GO LIVE WITH MY FRIEND KELLY.

GRAMMY ISN'T AS MUCH FUN AS SHE USED TO BE, AND I'M WONDERING WHAT I DID WRONG.

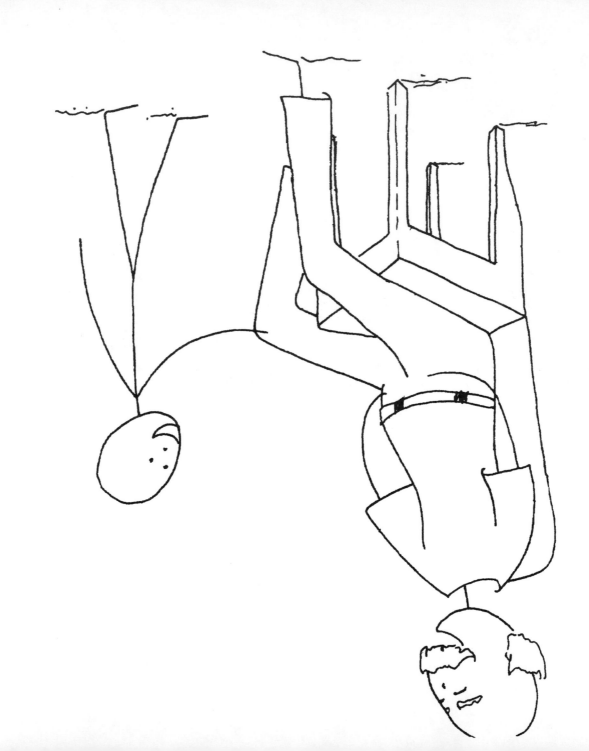

AND, Papa, WeLL, He's OKay.   We STiLL
TaLK aBOUT FUN THiNGS.

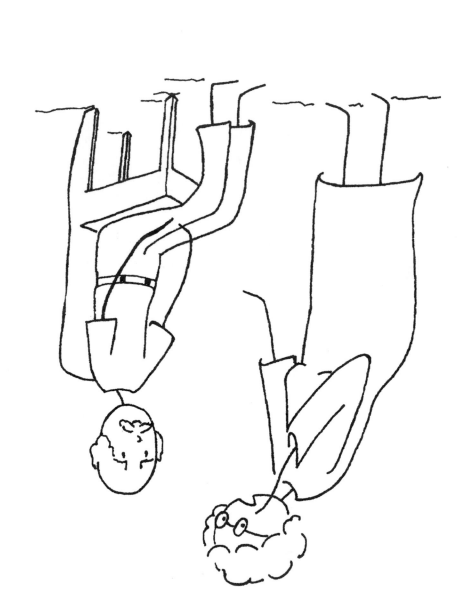
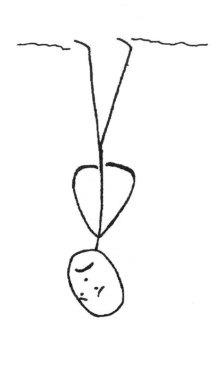

But, sometimes I hear Grammy say things to him (when I'm there and she doesn't know I can hear) that aren't very nice -- well, it's not that they aren't nice, they just don't feel very good. Papa doesn't say much, he just kind of grunts a little.

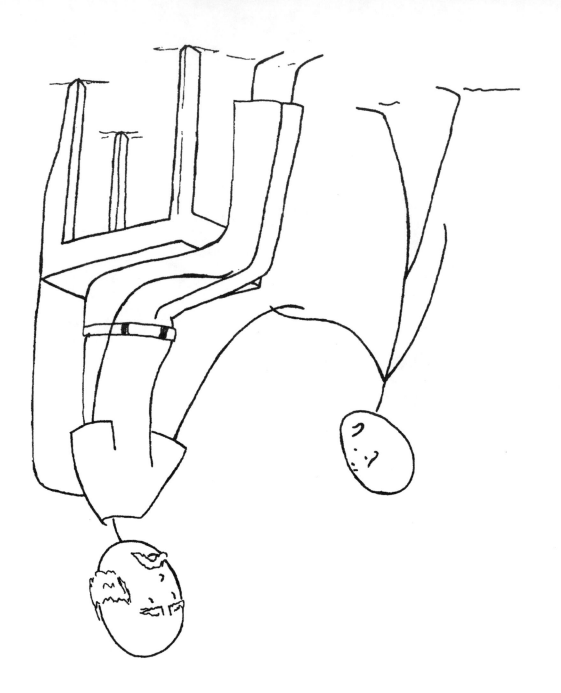

IT SCARES ME. I WISH I COULD TELL SOMEBODY.

I WISH I COULD JUST TELL THEM ALL TO GO BACK TO THE WAY THEY WERE.

I DON'T GET TO SEE GRANDMA AND GRANDPA AS MUCH AS I USED TO. I GUESS THEY DON'T LIKE ME SO MUCH NOW THAT DADDY DOESN'T LIVE HERE ANYMORE.

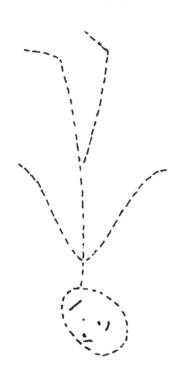

WHY CAN'T BIG PEOPLE GET ALONG? I HEARD MAMA SAY THEY USED TO BE SO HAPPY. WAS THAT BEFORE THEY HAD ME? I HEARD DADDY SAY HE NEVER DID DO ANYTHING RIGHT. THEY DON'T EVEN KNOW I'M AROUND SOMETIMES. I THINK I MUST BE INVISIBLE. I WISH I WERE.

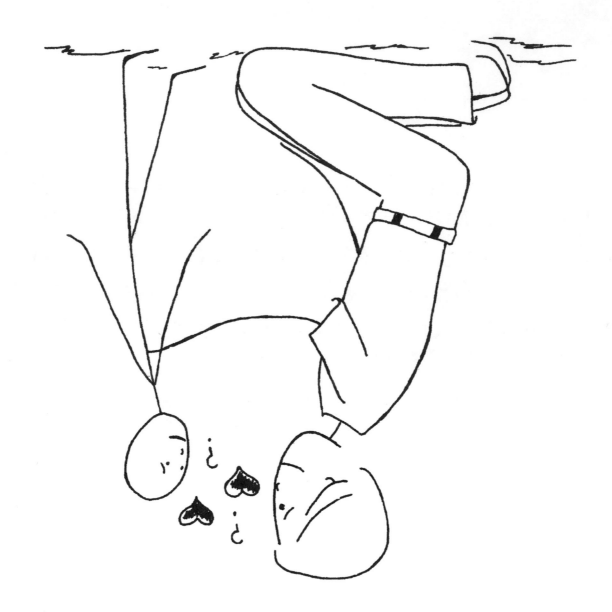

DaDDY Keeps asKiNG Me iF I STiLL Love Him. OH, He DOeSN'T Say iT JUST LiKe THaT, BUT I KNOW THaT'S WHaT He MeaNS. SOMeTiMeS We KiND OF aSK eaCH OTHeR THaT.

I THINK MAMA THINKS IF I STILL LIKE DADDY THAT I DON'T LIKE HER ANYMORE.

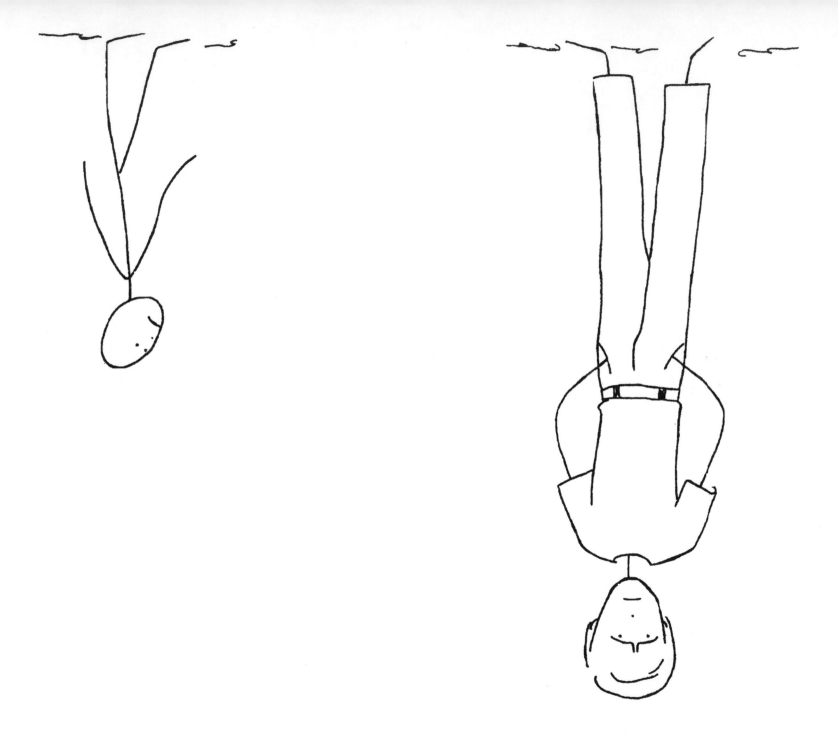

AND DADDY IS AFRAID THAT IF I STAY WITH MAMA OR GRAMMY THAT I WON'T LIKE HIM EITHER. I DON'T KNOW WHAT TO DO.

AND I'M AFRAID WHEN THEY GET SO ANGRY THAT THEY DON'T EITHER ONE LIKE ME ANYMORE.

IF I COULD JUST GO TO SLEEP AND WAKE UP IN THE MORNING AND HAVE DADDY HERE AND MAMA HAPPY AGAIN, I WOULD DO ANYTHING.

EPILOGUE

While the feelings you've just read about are very real and disturbing, there are remedies and actions which can be taken. Many opportunities exist for parents who wish to take action in assisting their children through this most difficult time.

For parents seeking help prior to divorcing or separating, many churches offer classes and/or counseling for both parents and children.

Many, many counselors provide marital and family counseling in virtually every moderate size community. For families whose incomes do not allow for the cost of individual counseling for either themselves or their children, there are many agencies which provide such services at reduced rates or without charge. These agencies, many of which are nonprofit, can be located in the yellow pages and some provide "hot" lines and one-on-one counseling for parents and/or children at no charge.

Other opportunities exist for group counseling for both adults (parents) and children. These are oftentimes held in church facilities or other community centers.

In many communities, it is required that divorcing parents of minor children participate in courses developed to provide information and insight into the world of their children before being granted the divorce. These courses are made available for a nominal fee from the parents with grant and sliding fee scale options for those whose incomes warrant it.

Whatever method you chose, it is imperative that children be considered, heard and helped through what may well be the most difficult event of their entire lives.

ORDER FORM
"BUT... WHAT ABOUT ME!"

NAME   PHONE NUMBER

ADDRESS

CITY   STATE   ZIP

NUMBER OF COPIES _____ @ $16.99 EA. = $ _____

PLUS SHIPPING/HANDLING_____ @ $ 2.00 EA. = $ _____

TEXAS RESIDENTS ADD 7.25% SALES TAX $ _____

CORPUS CHRISTI, TX RESIDENTS ADD 7.75% SALES TAX

TOTAL ENCLOSED	TOTAL	$ _____

OR YOU MAY CHARGE TO YOUR *DISCOVER®* CARD

X_____

CUSTOMER SIGNATURE   EXPIRATION DATE

MAKE CHECKS PAYABLE TO:

BOOKMARKPublishing

P.O. BOX 270636

CORPUS CHRISTI, TX 78427-0636

(512) 992-5814

FOR MORE INFORMATION, YOU MAY E-MAIL TO

BK@BOOKMARKPUBLISHING.COM

AND CHECK OUR WEBSITE: WWW.BOOKMARKPUBLISHING.COM

ORDER FORM
"But... What About Me!"

NAME _____ PHONE NUMBER _____

ADDRESS _____

CITY _____ STATE _____ ZIP _____

NUMBER OF COPIES _____ @ $16.99 EA. = $ _____
PLUS SHIPPING/HANDLING _____ @ $ 2.00 EA. = $ _____
TEXAS RESIDENTS ADD 7.25% SALES TAX $ _____
CORPUS CHRISTI, TX RESIDENTS ADD 7.75% SALES TAX

| TOTAL ENCLOSED | TOTAL | $ _____ |

OR YOU MAY CHARGE TO YOUR *DISCOVER*® CARD

X _____

CUSTOMER SIGNATURE   EXPIRATION DATE

MAKE CHECKS PAYABLE TO:

BOOKMARKPublishing
P.O. BOX 270636
CORPUS CHRISTI, TX 78427-0636
(512) 992-5814

FOR MORE INFORMATION, YOU MAY E-MAIL TO
BK@BOOKMARKPUBLISHING.COM
AND CHECK OUR WEBSITE: WWW.BOOKMARKPUBLISHING.COM